Linc

Lin

PA-Deitsh

Pennsylvania German

Story Book

Linda and Lilly

Lindi un Lilli

Original story by Madhav Chavan and

Manisha Vengurlekar

Illustrations by Santosh Pujari

Adapted by Karon Harden

and

D. Miller

Pennsylvania German
United States

Adaptation published by: STELLAR (STudents Empowered through Language, Literacy, and ARithmetic), American University of Nigeria, Lamido Zubairu Way, Yola By-Pass, Yola, Adamawa State, Nigeria PMB 2250, http://www.americanuniversitynigeria.org

This book is an adaptation and translation of Timmy and Pepe by Madhav Chavan and Manisha Vengurlekar, illustrated by Santosh Pujari

https://archive.org/download/PrathamBooks/Timmy-and-Pepe-English.pdf

Adapted and translated into Pennsylvania German

by: Deitsh Books
http://www.deitshbooks.com

Ich binn's Lindi.
Dess is mei friend, Lilli,
da glay hund.

Ich gleich shpeela
mitt di Lilli.
Ich sawk see vi miah's
saym sinn un vi miah
nett's saym sinn.

Di Lilli gleicht vann miah shpeela.

Ich sawk, "Gukk moll!
Ich habb en naws!"

"Woof!" sawkt di Lilli.
Sell maynd see hott
aw en naws.

Ich sawk, "Gukk moll!
Ich habb oahra!"

"Woof!" sawkt di Lilli.
Sell maynd see hott
aw oahra.

Ich sawk, "Gukk moll!
Ich habb awwa!"

"Woof!" sawkt di Lilli.
Sell maynd see hott
aw awwa.

Ich sawk, "Gukk moll!
Ich habb en zung!"

"Woof!" sawkt di Lilli.
Sell maynd see hott
aw en zung.

Ich sawk, "Gukk moll!
Ich habb bay!"

"Woof!" sawkt di Lilli.
Sell maynd see hott
aw bay.

Ich sawk, "Gukk moll!
Ich habb en kobb!"

"Woooof!" sawkt di Lilli.
Sell maynd see hott
aw en kobb.

Ich sawk, "Gukk moll!
Ich habb zvay hend!"

"Grrr..." sawkt di Lilli.
See drayt rumm un veist
iahra shvans. Sell maynd
see hott en shvans un
ich habb nett.

Avvah ich gleich di Lilli,
un di Lilli gleicht mich!

Kansht du sawwa vass
awl di diffahndi parts
funn dich sinn?

Vass sawkt in English!

1.
I am Linda.
This is my friend, Lilly, the puppy.

2.
I like to play with Lilly.
I tell her how we are the same and
how we are not the same.

3.
Lilly likes when we play.

4.
I say, "Look! I have a nose."

5.
"Woof!" says Lilly.
That means she has a nose too.

Vass sawkt in English!

6.
I say, "Look! I have ears."

7.
"Woof!" says Lilly.
That means she has ears too.

8.
I say, "Look! I have eyes."

9.
"Woof!" says Lilly.
That means she has eyes too.

10.
I say, "Look! I have a tongue."

Vass sawkt in English!

11.
"Woof!" says Lilly.
That means she has a tongue too.

12.
I say, "Look! I have legs."

13.
"Woof!" says Lilly.
That means she has legs too.

14.
I say, "Look! I have a head."

15.
"Woooof!" says Lilly.
That means she has a head too.

Vass sawkt in English!

16.
I say, "Look! I have two hands."

17.
"Grrr..." says Lilly.
She turns around and shows her tail.
That means she has a tail and I don't.

18.
But I love Lilly, and Lilly loves me!

19.
Can you name all your different
body parts?

Made in the USA
Columbia, SC
24 October 2017